THE MODEL T FORD

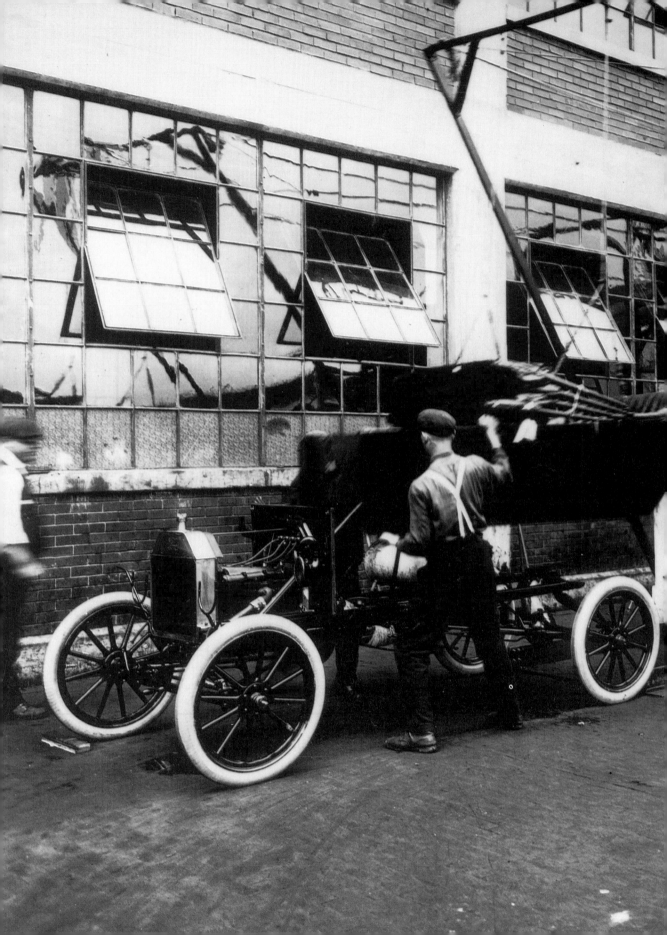

Turning Points
IN AMERICAN HISTORY

THE MODEL T FORD

Christopher Simonds

Silver Burdett Press, Inc.

Acknowledgments

The author and editor thank the following people for their invaluable help in text and picture research: Cheryl M. Crawford, Ford Motor Company; John Heilig, *Automobile Quarterly* magazine; Louis G. Helverson, the Free Library of Philadelphia; and Cynthia Read-Miller and Randy Mason, Henry Ford Museum and Greenfield Village.

Consultants

Elizabeth Blackmar
Assistant Professor
Department of History
Columbia College
New York, New York

Robert M. Goldberg
Consultant to the Social Studies Department
(formerly Department Chair)
Oceanside Middle School
Oceanside, New York

Cover: A worker installs engine parts on a Model T Ford in 1913. The Bettmann Archive.

Title Page: The moving assembly line at the Highland Park, Michigan, Ford factory in 1914. Corporate News Department, Ford Motor Company.

Contents Page: A red Model T touring car—from the days when the Model T was available in colors other than black. From the Collections of Hen Ford Museum and Greenfield Village.

Back Cover: A 1925 Model T advertisement shows a mailman making his rounds in bad weather with the aid of a Model T. From the Collections of Henry Ford Museum and Greenfield Village.

Library of Congress Cataloging-in-Publication Data

Simonds, Christopher.
    The Model T Ford / Christopher Simonds
        p.   cm — (Turning points in American history)
    Includes bibliographical references (p. 64) and index.
    Summary: Describes the development and production of the Ford
Model T car and its effects on America.
      1. Ford Model T automobile—Juvenile literature. [1. Ford Model.
    T automobile . 2. Automobiles—history.]   I. Title. II. Series.
    TL215.F75S56   1991
      629.222'2—dc20   91-13098
                                           CIP
                                           AC

Editorial Coordination by Richard G. Gallin

 Created by Media Projects Incorporated

Carter Smith, *Executive Editor*
Charles A. Wills, *Series Editor*
Bernard Schleifer, *Design Consultant*
Arlene Goldberg, *Cartographer*

ISBN 0-382-24122-3 [lib. bdg.]
10 9 8 7 6 5 4 3 2 1

ISBN 0-382-24117-7 [pbk.]
10 9 8 7 6 5 4 3 2 1

CONTENTS

INTRODUCTION

JUST ANOTHER CAR

On a warm September morning in 1908, Henry Ford left Detroit for a hunting trip to the back country of northern Michigan. He had been working long hours on a new project at the Ford Motor Company. Now it was time to relax. As more and more people were doing in those days, he and his companions traveled by automobile.

The road west to Chicago ran through Dearborn, the little farming town where Ford was born and had grown up. We don't know if he stopped to visit friends and relatives, or just honked and waved as his bright red car chugged along the dusty roads.

Only sixteen and a half hours later, the three men arrived in Chicago, 345 miles from Detroit. Their average speed for that leg of the trip was almost 21 miles an hour—fast for those days.

The next day they drove north along the shore of Lake Michigan to Milwau-kee. There they stopped to take in a twenty-four-hour auto race, then continued through the wooded wilderness of northern Wisconsin to Iron Mountain, Michigan.

While Ford stayed a few days in Iron Mountain, his partners drove the car back to Detroit. Rain had turned the dusty roads into rivers of mud. At one point, they had to make a dash through a brush fire. They took a faster route home, crossing Lake Michigan by ferry from Milwaukee.

The car reached Detroit on October 7, singed and caked with mud. It had burned sixty-eight gallons of gasoline and about twelve quarts of oil on the 1,357-mile trip. Except for a flat tire, it had had no mechanical problems at all.

Never in that long trip did the car attract attention or create excitement. By 1908, cars were a common sight on city streets and country roads. There were already about 200,000 cars in the nation, and more than two hundred companies were turning out more every day.

Henry Ford, creator of the Model T.

The Model T touring car—the most common model.

That automobile that took Ford hunting didn't look very different from the other cars of the day. It was boxier than most, and higher off the ground. The steering wheel was on the left, when most were still on the right. But all in all, it seemed like a fairly ordinary car.

Henry Ford knew better. That car was his dream come true—a simple, strong, dependable car at a price millions of people could afford. "The universal car," he called it. It was the first factory-produced Ford Model T. Over the next nineteen years, almost sixteen million more Model Ts would follow it onto the roads of the United States.

While Ford relaxed in the woods around Iron Mountain, the Ford Motor Company introduced the Model T to the public on October 1. For $850, the buyer got most of a car: The T had no top, no windshield, not even a spare tire.

From the first, Ford had only one problem with the Model T: making enough of them to meet demand. He knew that the more Ts he could make, the more he would sell. The more he sold, the lower he could bring the price. Every time the price went down, more people could afford the car.

Ford couldn't lose. Sure enough, the Model T made him a multimillionaire. More important, for better or worse, it put the United States on wheels.

1

HENRY FORD'S DREAM

No one person invented the automobile. It came about gradually from the work of dozens of people all over Europe and North America.

For decades before the first real, working automobile wobbled down a road, dreamers imagined it. They saw a vehicle that carried people swiftly from place to place down any road they chose, not just a road of rails. It used mechanical power, not muscle power like horse-drawn wagons or human-powered bicycles.

Steam-driven road vehicles were built in Britain, France, and the United States before 1800. They were heavy, slow, and impractical—a person on foot could make better time. Steam was fine for powering ship or railroad engines, but a steam motor small, light, and speedy enough to power a car wasn't

Henry Ford poses in his first car, the Quadricycle, on a Detroit street in 1896.

designed until late in the nineteenth century. By that time, a better power plant had arrived: the internal-combustion engine.

Internal combustion was a new idea. In a steam engine, wood, coal, or other fuel heats water. As the water turns to steam, it expands with great force. That force is used to turn wheels or do other work. The internal-combustion engine works differently: Fuel—usually gasoline—burns *inside* the engine. The energy released when it burns is turned directly into motion.

A Frenchman, Étienne Lenoir, built the first working internal combustion engine in 1860. His primitive engine was clumsy, like today's chain saw or weed-trimmer motors. The engine was attached to a road vehicle in Vienna, Austria, in 1863, but the experiment failed.

Other people improved on Lenoir's engine. A German, Nicholas Otto, was selling a hundred of his engines a

Carl Benz (center) and his family with two of Benz's early automobiles.

month by 1875. Then, in 1878, he patented an improved engine. The Otto engine was an instant success all over Europe, and by 1882 a version was being made and sold in the United States.

At first, the new gasoline engine was used as a *stationary engine*. It stayed bolted down in one place, running pumps, factory machinery, or farm equipment. In 1885, two German engineers, Karl Benz and Gottlieb Daimler, working separately, attached gasoline engines to wheeled vehicles. These primitive automobiles—Daimler's four-wheeler and Benz's three-wheeler—worked. A German newspaper wrote of the Benz machine: "It should prove quite useful to doctors, travelers, and lovers of sport."

It was in France with its smooth, level roads, not Germany with its primitive wagon tracks, that the automobile proved itself. The firm of Panhard & Levassor bought the French rights to make the Daimler engine. They put the engines on carriages, in front of the driver, not under the seat as Daimler and Benz had. Sales of the new vehicles were good, other companies sprang up, and by the early 1900s horse-drawn carriages were sharing the streets of Paris with *les automobiles*.

This lithograph from the 1870s celebrates the United States's mechanical progress, including the railroad and the telegraph.

Driving around on paved city streets was one thing, serious travel was another. Long-distance races proved that the auto wasn't yet up to the challenge of the open road. In 1894, a steam-powered car won a 50-mile race in France; gas vehicles came in second and fourth. The next year, however, a Panhard & Levassor came in first in a 727-mile race from Paris to Bordeaux and back again.

All this activity in Europe didn't go unnoticed in the United States. The nation had celebrated its one-hundredth birthday in 1876. Now, everyone agreed, the country was in the machine age. Steam locomotives pulled trains at speeds of over one hundred miles an hour. Machines—many powered by gas engines—were everywhere, doing everything. They washed clothes, harvested crops, peeled apples, drilled tunnels, swept floors, and lit cities. They spun cotton and wool into yarn, wove yarn into cloth, and sewed cloth into clothing. They made pins and cannons, buttons and battleships. There was nothing people did, it seemed, that a machine could not do faster, more cheaply, and more easily.

Magazines in the United States published articles about Otto's engine and

The "motor wagon"—one of the Duryea brothers' early cars.

about Daimler's and Benz's automobiles. All over the nation, in country barns and in city sheds, mechanics began tinkering with gasoline engines and horseless carriages. One of them, but by no means the first, was a young engineer in Detroit, Michigan—Henry Ford.

The first Americans to build a gasoline automobile that actually ran were two bicycle mechanics, Charles and Frank Duryea. As a high school student, Charles wrote a paper on "Transportation Other Than Rails." Among other ideas, his paper suggested that someday flying machines would cross the Atlantic Ocean in less than a day.

When the Duryeas tried out their car, in September 1893, they were delighted. It ran—at the then amazing speed of eighteen miles per hour. Others were not far behind. Elwood Haynes of Kokomo, Indiana, tested his first car on July 4, 1894. A maker of gasoline engines, Ransom E. Olds, had a car running in 1896; so did Alexander Winton. And then there was Henry Ford.

Machinery fascinated Ford. Born in 1863 and raised on a farm in Dearborn, Michigan, about ten miles from Detroit, he grew up like most country boys. He went to school, helped on the farm, and played with his friends when he could find the time. But farm life was really not for him. "There was too much work on the place," he recalled later. "Even when I was very young, I suspected that much might be done in a better way."

A better, easier way of doing things called for mechanical contraptions. One of Ford's first was a gate opener that took away the bother of having to climb down from horse or wagon, open a gate, then climb back on. Another was a little water-powered mill he and his friends built. It worked, but unfortunately it flooded a neighbor's potato field.

Then there were watches. Young Ford loved watches. Legend says he took his father's watch apart to see how it worked and got himself a whipping. In fact, William Ford was patient with his son's tinkering ways. Henry would settle down in time, his father believed, and grow up to be a fine farmer. A boyhood friend later recalled that when still a schoolboy, Ford could take a broken watch apart—then put it back together, running as good as new.

The summer he was twelve, Ford discovered a new machine much more exciting than a watch. It lumbered down a country road, hissing and chugging: a steam engine running not on rails but on a road. In fact, this engine was not meant for transportation. It had just enough speed and power to go from farm to farm, where it was used as a stationary engine to do farm work like threshing wheat. Nevertheless, it got young Ford thinking.

Henry Ford as a young boy.

During the months that followed, Ford got to know the engine well. Its owner, Fred Reden, let the boy feed it coal, oil it, and eventually drive it. Ford quickly understood how the tangle of pistons, shafts, gears, and pulleys worked together to move the engine. Most probably, getting acquainted with Fred Reden's engine ended any chance of Henry Ford's becoming a sober, sensible Michigan farmer.

Five years later, in 1879, Ford packed his bags and left home for Detroit. There he worked in several machine shops and added to his wages by repairing watches at night. As he later recalled, a thought came to him: With the right machinery, he could make 2,000 watches a day. If he made them in that quantity, he could price them at 30 cents apiece and still make a profit. But this was followed by another thought: Would he be able to *sell* 2,000 watches a day? Probably not, and so the Ford Watch Company died before it was born. "Even then," Ford wrote later, "I wanted to make something in quantity."

Ford put his experience to work in 1882, when he became a field engineer for the Westinghouse Company. He traveled all over Michigan, setting up and repairing the company's steam wheat threshers and other products. In 1885, he met a quiet, pretty girl named Clara Bryant—like Ford, the child of a successful Michigan farmer. He fell in love with her, perhaps because she was willing to go for a ride with him—on a steam thresher.

They married in 1888, and Henry looked for work that would not take him away from home. He found a job with the Edison Illuminating Company in Detroit, at $45 a week. During the day, he tended the giant machines that generated electric power for the city. At night, he spent hours in the shed behind the Ford house, building a gasoline engine.

Nobody knows when Ford decided to build an automobile. The idea probably didn't come to him in a sudden

As a boy, Henry Ford loved to experiment with mechanical things—especially watches, as shown in this painting from the 1920s.

Henry and Clara Ford preparing the gasoline engine for Henry Ford's first automobile.

flash. Like any American of the 1890s, Ford had waited for late trains, ridden in crowded, smelly trolley cars, dealt with stubborn horses, and walked until his feet cried in pain. Again like most people of his time, he believed in mechanical progress—that machines would keep on making life easier and better. From reading newspapers and popular science magazines, he knew people had built cars in Europe and were trying to build them in the United States.

Whatever may have inspired Ford, we know that by Christmas Eve 1894 he had a gasoline motor ready to run. He brought it from the shed into the kitchen and bolted it to the sink. While their baby son, Edsel, slept in the next room, Clara Ford dribbled gasoline into the engine while Henry Ford spun a fly-wheel that created a spark which ignited the gas. The motor coughed, sputtered, and roared into life.

The motor was the easy part. It took Ford another two and a half years to get his automobile on the road. There were many problems to solve: how to get the gasoline into the combustion chamber, how to send the engine's power to the driving wheels, and how to stop the car once it was moving.

On June 4, 1896, Ford was ready. The car was too big to pass through the shed

Henry Ford rolls out his first car on the morning of June 4, 1896.

door, Ford's landlord remembered years later, so Ford took a sledgehammer and knocked out a larger opening. At four o'clock in the morning, he rolled the car into his backyard.

It was not an impressive machine. It looked like a large box with a bicycle wheel at each corner. There was no seat, and the driver steered with a long handle like the tiller of a boat. But it worked: It started and went putt-putting down the alley out into the empty streets. The noisy engine may have made Ford's neighbors stir in their sleep, but no crowds gathered for the historic moment.

The Quadricycle—the car that launched Henry Ford on his career as a builder of automobiles.

In the days that followed, Henry Ford's car became a familiar sight on the streets of Detroit. Now crowds did gather. "If I left it alone even for a minute," Ford reported, "some person always tried to run it. Finally, I had to carry a chain and chain it to a lamp post whenever I left it anywhere."

Later that summer, Henry Ford drove the car to the Dearborn farm where he grew up. Clara rode at his side, holding Edsel firmly on her lap. They visited friends and family. William Ford was pleasant enough, but he didn't seem greatly impressed with his son Henry's first car.

Ford HIGH PRICED QUALITY IN A LOW PRICED CAR

The Ford Four Cylinder, Twenty Horse Power, Five Passenger Touring Car $850 00 Fob. Detroit

THE one real automobile value among all the "season sensation" announcements is this big, roomy, powerful five-passenger touring car at the hitherto unheard of price of $850.00. A car that possesses at least equal value with any "1909" car announced, and at the same time sells for several hundred dollars less than the lowest of the rest.

Compare the following features of the new Ford car with those of any higher priced car offered and see if you can justify in your own mind the additional expenditure that buying any other car involves.

The Model T is a 4-cylinder, 20 h. p., five-passenger family car—powerful, speedy and enduring,—a car that looks good and is as good as it looks. Built in our own shops, it is not an "assembled" car.

It is supplied with a unit power plant—and the magneto is an integral part of same, a guaranteed troubleless magneto,—cylinders are cast in one block with detachable head, rendering all parts easily accessible.

A 3-bearing crank shaft insures perfect alignment. A cam shaft with 8 cams integral, guarantees proper valve operation. Crank and cam shafts drop-forged, each from a single non-welded Vanadium steel ingot.

Steering gear on left-hand side,—the logical side for American roads.

Car is shaft driven through one universal joint to Ford system of final drive. Patented in all countries. The system acknowledged to be the only adequate solution of the problem of delivering power to the wheels.

Vanadium steel is used throughout the entire car wherever strength is necessary. The axles, shafts, connecting rods, springs, gears, brackets, etc., are all of Vanadium steel,—each from a separate formula and all especially heat-treated in our own plant and from our own analyses. We defy anyone to break a Ford Vanadium steel part with any test or strain less than 50% greater than is required to put any other special automobile steel entirely out of business.

The weight of the car is only 1,200 lbs.—brought about by scientific construction and the use of Vanadium steel. Not an ounce of necessary weight sacrificed, not an ounce of dead weight in the car.

The importance of this light weight is vast. M. Michelin, noted tire expert, in a paper recently read before the French Society of Civil Engineers, said: "The total travel of which a tire is capable is inversely proportional to the cube of the weight which it carries." If the load is doubled the average wear and tear is multiplied by eight, if the weight of the car is increased $33\frac{1}{3}$% the life of the tire is decreased one-half. The effect on gasoline and oil consumption and the need for repairs is similar.

That is one of the reasons the Ford car will run more miles for less money than any other touring car manufactured.

One-hundred-inch wheel base, 56-inch tread, 30-inch wheels, $3\frac{1}{2}$-inch tire rear, 3-inch front; gasoline capacity, 10 gallons—225 to 250 miles; long, clean-cut lines throughout, handsomely finished, and you have the specifications on the real automobile value of this year and next and a couple more thereafter.

We make no apologies for the price,—any car now selling up to several hundred dollars more could, if built from Ford design, in the Ford factory, by Ford methods, and in Ford quantities, be sold for the Ford price if the makers were satisfied with the Ford profit per car.

Your guarantee that this car is all we claim—and our claims are broad—is in the reputation of Henry Ford, who never designed or built a failure, and in the reputation of the Ford Motor Company, who have built $20,000,000.00 worth of successful cars of Ford design in the same factory, with the same organization and system, and bearing the same imprint that the Model T is manufactured under. It's the guarantee of works as well as words.

Delivery began October 1st, orders filled in rotation. Cars can be seen at all branch stores; get a demonstration if you are near by, if not, wire your order either for immediate shipment or definite future delivery.

FURTHER details in catalog, which is yours for the asking.

Ford Motor Company
266 Piquette Ave.
Detroit

BRANCHES:—
New York, Boston, Philadelphia, Buffalo, Cleveland, Chicago, St. Louis, Kansas City, Denver, Seattle.
Paris, France. London, England. Canadian Trade:—Ford Motor Company, of Canada, Ltd. Walkerville Ont. Branch, Toronto.

Ford

2

~~~~~~

A CAR FOR EVERYONE

Between 1892 and 1896, the first American automobiles chugged, one at a time, out of barns, blacksmith shops, and backyard sheds like Henry Ford's. As the proud owner-builders drove down city streets and up country roads, other Americans took notice. It was hard to ignore this noisy, fast-moving new gadget. A few people were fascinated; many were mildly curious; some were out-and-out hostile. Curiosity was natural, and hostility was understandable: The gasoline buggies frightened horses, ran over livestock, and coated washing hung out to dry with road dust. But the auto caught the imagination of people who didn't have the money or the mechanical knack to build one but nevertheless wanted a car of their own.

By 1900, the automobile was no

This advertisement for the Ford Model T—the very first—appeared early in 1909.

longer a tinkerer's toy. In less than a decade, it had become an industrial product. The Duryea brothers were the first to manufacture cars for sale. Their Duryea Motor Company, founded in 1895, sold the first American gasoline car early in 1896. Ransom E. Olds began selling cars the same year. The Winton Motor Carriage Company followed in 1897, and the Haynes-Apperson Company in 1898. By 1899, thirty manufacturers were in business. They made 2,500 gasoline, steam, and electric vehicles that year.

The time was ripe for the gasoline-powered automobile. American mines and mills could supply all the iron and steel automobile makers needed. The rubber industry was ready to provide tires, thanks to the "bicycle boom" of the 1880s and 1890s, when many people took up bicycle riding as a sport or a means of transportation.

The need for fuel to run the cars also

AND THE WINNER IS . . . GASOLINE!

The Pope Manufacturing Company of Hartford, Connecticut, was the nation's leading maker of bicycles. Shortly before 1900, the firm decided to build automobiles as well—but what kind? Steam, electric, or gasoline? Shown a test model of a gasoline-powered car, a Pope executive shook his head sadly and said: "We are on the wrong track. No one will buy a carriage that has to have all that greasy machinery in it."

He was almost right. In the automobile's infant years, the gasoline-powered internal-combustion engine was not the only choice. Vehicles powered by steam and electricity were also popular. In 1900, in the United States, 4,192 cars were built. Of these, 1,681 were steam-driven, 1,575 were electric, and only 936 had internal-combustion engines. In that year, the biggest-selling American vehicle was the Locomobile #2, a little steamer selling for the very low price of $750. Three years earlier, electric taxicabs had appeared on the streets of New York; in 1898, Pope turned out 500 electric cars.

Steam and electricity offered many advantages over the noisy, smelly internal-combustion engine, which shook and shuddered even when the car was standing still. Both were quiet: An electric made no noise at all, while a steamer speeding down the road gave off a gentle *chuffa-chuffa-chuffa*. Both rode smoothly—if the driver could find a smooth road. With fewer moving parts to wear out or break, steam and electric cars were more reliable than the "gas buggies." Both accelerated smoothly from a dead stop to top speed; neither required the driver to shift gears.

Electrics were poky, with top speeds around 30 miles per hour, but steam cars were speedy. In 1906, on a flat Florida beach, a Stanley Steamer did a mile in 28.2 seconds—over 127 miles per hour—a record that stood for four years. In that race, Henry Ford's brand-new, 105-horsepower gasoline racer broke down and did not finish.

In spite of these and other advantages, steam and electric cars were mostly out of the picture by 1910. In that year 200,000 cars were made in the United States, all but 5,000 of them powered by internal-combustion engines burning gasoline.

Electric cars never caught on because, except in large cities, they were impractical. They needed huge, heavy lead-acid batteries to turn their wheels. The batteries had to be recharged every twenty-five miles or so, meaning that the driver could never travel far from a recharging station. Recharging took two to three hours. Worse, batteries wore out quickly and had to be replaced. It cost two to three cents a mile to run an electric; a gas vehicle cost its owner less than a penny a mile.

A 1910 Stanley Steamer.

Steam cars could outrun and outclimb gasoline vehicles, but they also had serious disadvantages. Steamers used gasoline or kerosene to heat water. As the water turned to steam, it expanded, driving pistons that turned the wheels. Though few steamers actually exploded, many people felt nervous sitting on top of a high-pressure boiler.

Because the steamer had to carry both fuel and a large supply of water, it was heavy; its weight made it a fuel guzzler. Worse, water had to be added every thirty miles or so; then the driver had to wait fifteen to thirty minutes for pressure to build up. And any old water would not do: Impure water quickly clogged the boiler tubes, making major repairs necessary.

Internal combustion cars were cheaper to buy and cheaper to run than steamers or electrics. They could go anywhere: An early Ford with its 10-gallon tank, getting 20 miles to the gallon, had a range of 200 miles. Most any country store sold gasoline ("stove gas," it was called then). Gas vehicles may have broken down more often, but they were easier to repair than the other types.

The years from 1900 to 1910 saw great technical progress in the auto industry. Gas vehicles became faster, safer, cheaper, and more reliable. Steam and electric vehicles improved too. Lighter, longer-lasting batteries appeared that had to be recharged less often. New quick-heating boilers did away with the long wait for steam pressure to build up. But by the time these improvements were in place, the buying public had voted, and the gasoline internal-combustion engine had won.

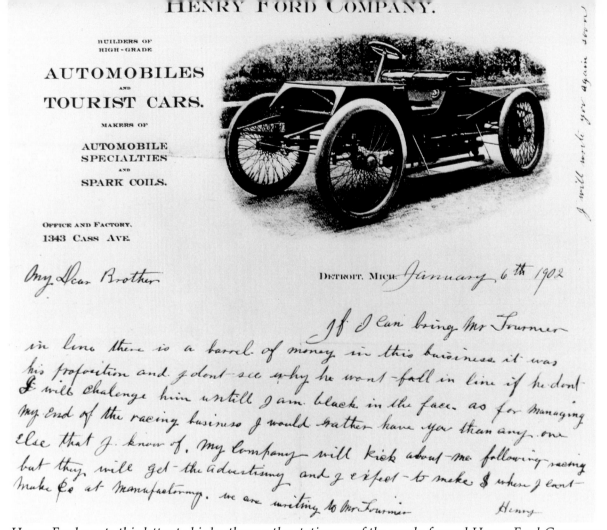

BUILDERS OF
HIGH-GRADE

AUTOMOBILES
AND
TOURIST CARS.

MAKERS OF

AUTOMOBILE
SPECIALTIES
AND

SPARK COILS.

OFFICE AND FACTORY.
1343 CASS AVE.

My Dear Brother

DETROIT. MICH. January, 6th 1902

If I can bring Mr Fournier in line there is a barrel of money in this business it was his proposition and I dont see why he wont fall in line if he dont I will chalenge him untill I am black in the face. as for managing my end of the racing business I would rather have you than any one else that I know of. My company will kick about me following racing but they will get the advertising and I expect to make $ when I cant make $ at manufactorung. we are writing to Mr Fournier

Henry

Henry Ford wrote this letter to his brother on the stationery of the newly formed Henry Ford Company.

saved the American oil industry. Until the 1890s, gasoline was a waste product left over when crude oil was refined into kerosene, which was used to light lamps. When Thomas Edison made the first electric light in 1879, it was the beginning of the end for the oil lamp. But as kerosene sales dropped, demand for gasoline rose. Refiners adjusted quickly, producing more gasoline and less kerosene.

Finally, railroad lines crisscrossed the United States. A manufacturer could build automobiles in one central factory and ship them quickly and cheaply anywhere in the country.

Henry Ford sold his first car, the one he built in the woodshed in 1896, for $200. He needed the money to build an improved model. In 1899, he quit his job with the Edison company. With financial backing from Detroit Mayor William Maybury and others, Ford organized the Detroit Automobile Company. The company sold its first vehicle, a delivery wagon, in January 1900. About twenty more cars followed, but by the end of the year the firm was out of business. Ford blamed the failure on his backers' desire for quick profits. The backers blamed Ford. He was a perfectionist,

AUTOMOBILES RICHARD-BRASIER

GAGNANTES DE LA COUPE GORDON BENNETT 1904

SOCIÉTÉ DES ANCIENS ÉTABLISSEMENTS GEORGES RICHARD

23, Avenue de la GRANDE ARMÉE   PARIS

A PRIZE-WINNING RACING CAR, *led by a wind-blown spirit of speed, was featured in this Parisian advertisement by Eugène Verneau.*

Auto racing was popular in Europe before it came to the United States. This 1904 poster advertises a French car that won the important Gordon Bennett trophy.

they charged, forever fiddling with mechanical details when he should be turning out cars to bring in money.

Late in 1901, Ford found new investors and formed the Henry Ford Company. History repeated itself: The new company made very few cars, and Ford left in March 1902. The company was reorganized and brought out a new car, the Cadillac. His partners, Ford said later, wanted to build expensive cars to order. The company was "merely a money-making concern that did not make much money." Ford had a better idea. He wanted to build a reliable, inexpensive car—and build it in large quantities, to keep the selling price low.

During this period, Ford took a step that had little to do with building a practical car for common people but brought him plenty of publicity. He began racing cars.

In 1895, inspired by that year's Paris-Bordeaux race in France, the Chicago *Times-Herald* sponsored the first American race, which took place in November. The course was fifty-four miles from Chicago to Evanston, Illinois, and back. Running in foot-deep snow and averaging eight miles per hour, an American-built Duryea beat two imported Benzes.

Given the primitive roads of the day, point-to-point races were tests of the

Race driver Barney Oldfield at the wheel of the Ford 999. Henry Ford is standing next to the car.

cars' endurance, not their speed. By 1896, car builders and drivers were competing for speed records on oval dirt tracks. In the first such race, at Narragansett, Rhode Island, in September 1896, a Ricker electric outran five Duryeas, reaching a speed of just under twenty-seven miles per hour. This didn't impress the audience: For the first time, the soon-familiar taunt "Get a horse!" was heard.

In the next few years, speed records were made one weekend and broken the next. When Ford turned to racing, Alexander Winton's enormous Bullet held the U.S. record with a mile in 1:14.5. On October 10, 1901, Ford drove his 26-horsepower, two-cylinder racer, which came from behind to beat the Bullet and set a new record, 1:12.4—just under fifty miles per hour.

Ford next built two 70-horsepower monsters, 999 and The Arrow. He did not drive them himself: "The roar of those cylinders alone," he said, "was enough to half kill a man." Instead, he hired bicycle racing star Barney Oldfield, who had never driven an automobile. In his first outing, Oldfield beat Winton and set a new speed record, a mile in 1:06. Two years later, Ford set a speed record of his own, driving a racer at 91.4 miles per hour on the ice of Lake St. Clair.

Seeing its publicity value, Ford kept racing until 1907. At the Michigan State Fair that year, he watched in horror as his new six-cylinder racer skidded and

The 1903 Ford Model A.

turned two somersaults, hurling driver Frank Kulick through the air. Ford drove Kulick to the hospital (miraculously, the driver survived) and never built a racing car again.

Ford's venture into racing helped build his reputation as a maker of durable cars. That image helped make his third business, the Ford Motor Company, a success. He founded Ford Motor in June 1903. Financial backing came from Alexander Malcomson, a coal dealer. Malcomson rounded up nine other investors, including the Dodge brothers, Horace and John, who promised to build engines for Ford.

The Ford Motor Company was one of fifty-seven firms to start making automobiles in 1903. In the same year,

thirty manufacturers went out of business. Ford was nearly one of them: On July 11, the company's bank balance was down to $223.65. In the nick of time, a check for $850 arrived, payment for the company's first car—a Model A ordered by a Chicago doctor.

By the end of March 1904, Ford had sold 658 Model As; a year later, three hundred workers were turning out twenty-five of the trim little red cars a day. The Model A, Ford's advertisements said, was "built to take you anywhere you want to go and get you back again on time." The car was not at all luxurious, but the price was right: $850 for a simple, reliable, 8-horsepower car. That price, about a year's pay for a skilled worker, was within the reach of

Henry Ford and his son Edsel in a Ford Model C in 1905.

professional people like doctors, lawyers, small business owners, and others in the growing middle class. For those who wanted a little more power, Ford made the $900 Model C and the $1,200 Model F. The C was an enlarged A with the engine moved to the front and beefed up to 10 horsepower. The Model F boasted 12 horsepower. Sales of the A, C, and F rose steadily, but as always, Ford wanted more. In May 1905, he told reporters he intended to make 10,000 cars a year and sell them for $400 apiece.

To Henry Ford's annoyance, his company also made the Model B. The B was Malcomson's baby: a big car, more luxurious than the A, with a four-cylinder engine that produced 24 horsepower. The B cost $2,000, much less than other luxury models, but it went against Henry Ford's desire to build a simple, inexpensive "universal car." He liked the Model K, a six-cylinder successor to the B, even less.

Ford was secretly pleased when the B and the $2,800 K proved to be money losers. Overall, because of the success of Models A, C, and F, the company was doing well. In 1905, sales totaled $1.9 million, and the stockholders—Ford, Malcomson, the Dodges, and a handful of others—divided $200,000 in profits.

The running battle with Malcomson

The 1906 Ford Model N—a simple, inexpensive car that was the Model T's direct ancestor.

strengthened Ford's belief that sharing control with partners was not for him. He didn't have to look far for more evidence. In 1903, Ransom E. Olds, a pioneer of the auto industry, was pushed out of his own company by partners who wanted to build big, costly cars for the luxury market. Ford knew that Olds had made the company successful by building a simple runabout, the "curved-dash Oldsmobile," in large quantities and selling it at the reasonable price of $695. Olds was the first carmaker to mass-produce cars rather than build them one at a time. The company survived without Olds, but just barely.

Ford decided to get rid of Malcomson. Late in 1905, he and some like-minded Ford stockholders formed the Ford Manufacturing Company. The new company's sole purpose was to build engines and frames for the new Model N and sell them to Ford Motor. A big slice of future Ford Motor profits would thus go to Ford Manufacturing, leaving Malcomson out in the cold. In a rage, he quit as a director of Ford Motor, sold his stock back to Ford, and founded the Aerocar Company, which never amounted to much. Now that Henry Ford and those who thought as he did controlled the company, Ford never again had to build a car he didn't believe in.

The Model N, like the A before it, was an inexpensive, reliable car. It had a bigger engine than the A, with 15 horsepower and four cylinders instead of two.

Priced at $600, the N was the first

four-cylinder, four-passenger car to sell for under $1,000. "In making the price on this four-cylinder runabout," an advertisement said, "the question was not, 'How much can we get for this car?' but 'How low can we sell it and make a small margin [profit] on each one?'"

Though it lacked a top and a windshield, the Model N had several improvements over earlier Fords, including a better drive shaft and an emergency brake. Buyers who wanted a little more horsepower, or extras like horns and lights, could buy the Model R or S, both based on the N.

Ford made 10,000 of the new cars and sold them as fast as they could be turned out. The company prospered, and at the end of 1907 the directors raised Henry Ford's salary to $36,000 a year. That was high pay in those days, but it was peanuts compared with the value of Henry Ford's stock in his company. Not quite a year later, he and the other stockholders shared a dividend of $1,900,000 from the company's profits. Employees, too, shared in Ford's success: In 1908, workers who had been with the company two years or more got bonuses of 7.5 percent of their annual earnings—a "gift from the company" of $50 or more.

In the summer of 1908, work began on the Ford Motor Company's new factory in Highland Park, just outside Detroit. It was as long as three football fields and four stories high—the world's largest automobile plant and the largest building in Michigan. Ford needed this new factory to produce his new car: the Model T.

Work on the T began in 1907, in the "experimental room" next to Henry Ford's office. There Ford sat for hours, in a rocking chair that had once belonged to his grandmother, facing a large blackboard. Every part of the new car was sketched on the blackboard by Ford's engineers and machinists. Ford would suggest improvements; then the part would be handmade and tested. "Let's start it up," Ford said at one point, "and see why it doesn't work."

By March 1908, Ford Motor announced that the T would go into production that fall and that 25,000 of the new cars would be built in the first year. The announcement gave few details of the new model, but the public believed Henry Ford couldn't miss. All through the spring and summer of 1908, orders poured in for what the company called "the car that any man can own, who can afford a horse and carriage."

"A limited number of factories can supply all the demand for high-priced cars," Henry Ford said as the T was being built, "but the market for a low-priced car is unlimited."

The first Model T was hand-built in the summer of 1908, tested, then taken apart so all the parts could be checked. During the testing, Henry Ford was jubilant. He laughed, joked, slapped his workers on the back, and drove past Alexander Malcomson's office, loudly tooting the horn.

The Model T was not a radically new and different car. It was more powerful and simpler to operate than the Model N. The most obvious change from earlier Fords and most other American cars was that the steering wheel was on the left, where it has stayed ever since. The car was light—under 1,200 pounds—which made for better gas mileage and less wear on expensive tires. Ford also used a new kind of steel that made the T's moving parts lighter and longer-wearing.

Ford made the car as simple as he could. When the company supplying carburetors—the device that mixes gasoline and air to be burned in the combustion chamber—showed him a model held together by sixteen bolts, he looked at it and returned it. Too many parts, Ford said. The supplier improved the design, bringing down the number of bolts to two. Again Ford rejected it. The supplier finally produced a carburetor held together by one bolt.

A two-passenger Model T runabout cost $825, and a four-passenger (five, if those in the backseat squeezed) touring car sold for $850. Headlights, folding top, windshield, and spare tire were extra-cost options. For his money, the buyer got a car that was easy to drive, seldom broke down, and cruised at forty miles per hour—well over the speed limits of the day. Gas mileage was twenty-two to twenty-five miles per gallon.

Production was slow at first. In October 1908, Ford made eight Ts, all of which were sent to Europe for display. By the end of the year, 309 had been built. But by May 1, 1909, Ford's future output of Ts through August was already sold, and by mid-June, 2,190 Ford workers had built 10,660 of the new cars. That year, Ford pulled ahead of

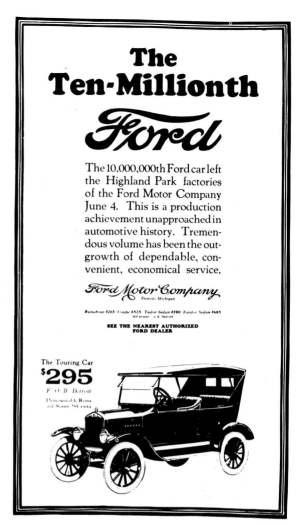

This 1924 advertisement celebrates the ten-millionth Model T.

Buick to become the nation's biggest car manufacturer.

In the years that followed, sales soared—and as they did, prices dropped, bringing the Model T within the reach of more and more Americans. The one-millionth Model T rolled out of the factory in December 1915. By then, the price of a touring car was down to $440. The all-time low price, $290, came in December 1924. Two and a half years later, the last Model T, Number 15,458,781, was built. Henry Ford had put the United States on wheels.

Her habit of measuring time in terms of dollars gives the woman in business keen insight into the true value of a Ford closed car for her personal use.

This car enables her to conserve minutes, to expedite her affairs, to widen the scope of her activities. Its low first cost, long life and inexpensive operation and upkeep convince her that it is a sound investment value.

And it is such a pleasant car to drive that it transforms the business call which might be an interruption into an enjoyable episode of her busy day.

TUDOR SEDAN, $590   FORDOR SEDAN, $685   COUPE, $525   (All prices f. o. b. Detroit)

Ford
CLOSED CARS

May 1924 Good Housekeeping

3

AMERICA TAKES THE WHEEL

Who bought the cars Henry Ford and others built? At first, most Americans brushed off the automobile as a fad, a "rich man's toy"—and at first, they were right. Before 1900, wealthy Americans bought magnificent cars, usually imported from Europe. A long, gleaming, powerful car became a "status symbol"—a sign of the owner's wealth and social standing. Millionaires drove (or were driven by their chauffeurs) to and from one another's estates, where they played motor polo on the lawns and angered ordinary folks by racing on quiet country roads. John Jacob Astor, the multimillionaire, owned thirty-two cars shortly after 1900.

Imported cars and big American luxury cars cost up to $7,500. Even most

This Ford advertisement from the early 1920s was aimed at a new kind of customer—the businesswoman.

American-built cars cost $2,000 or more in those years. This was at a time when clerks, shopkeepers, and teachers made $600 to $900 a year, and the average factory worker was paid less than $10 per week.

Soon, however, the automobile attracted buyers who were well off but not fabulously rich. The first to give up the horse for the car were doctors. In a curved-dash Olds or Ford Model A, a country doctor of 1903 could cover 75 to 100 miles a day, compared with 40 or 50 miles in a horse-drawn buggy. The doctor could visit more patients and respond more quickly in emergencies. Unlike a horse, a car did not get tired or sick. It was always ready to go.

Engineers whose work took them into the field found the automobile useful. It carried traveling salesmen to new territories away from the railroads. Though some preachers blasted the

CARS OF 1908

In 1908, the year the Model T Ford was born, more than two hundred U.S. companies made automobiles (or claimed to—some were "paper companies" that never scraped up enough money to actually build cars). Some of the more popular cars of that time were:

Acme	DeLuxe	Marmon	Pope-Toledo
American Traveler	Elmore	Matheson	Premier
American Locomotive	EMF	Maxwell	Pullman
Anderson	Ford	Mercer	Rainier
Apperson	Franklin	Mitchell	Rambler
Atlas	Frazer-Miller	Moline	Regal
Auburn	Frontenac	Moon	Reo
Austin	Gearless	Mora	Simplex
Autocar	Glide	Northern	Speedwell
Baker Electric	Gyroscope	Oakland	Stanley Steamer
Brush	Haynes	Oldsmobile	Stearns
Buick	Holsman	Overland	Stevens-Duryea
Cadillac	Hupmobile	Packard	Stoddard-Dayton
Cartercar	Imperial	Palmer	Waltham
Chalmers-Detroit	Jackson	Peerless	Walton
Cleveland	Knox	Pennsylvania	Welch
Columbia	Locomobile	Pierce Arrow	White
Corbin	Lozier	Pope-Hartford	Winton

Some changed their names. Oakland became Pontiac; EMF was later called Studebaker. Rambler became Nash, which in turn became American Motors and was eventually taken over by the Chrysler Corporation in the late 1980s.

Other companies merged. Cadillac, Oldsmobile, Buick, and Oakland combined into General Motors, which introduced the Chevrolet—the car that killed the Model T—in the 1920s.

The Great Depression that began in 1929 finished off many automobile companies. A few—Nash, Studebaker, Packard—lingered on after World War II. Reo and White survived a while longer, as builders of trucks. But in the 1950s and 1960s—the "golden age" of the American automobile, before foreign manufacturers invaded the United States with their Volkswagens, Toyotas, and Saabs—almost all American cars came from the "Big Three": Chrysler (formed in the 1920s), General Motors, and Ford.

auto as an invention of the Devil, others saw that with a car, one minister could cover two or three churches. Merchants began using motorized delivery wagons to better serve their customers. City governments adopted the auto: Police in Akron, Ohio, had an automobile patrol wagon in 1898, and by 1903 several eastern cities began using horseless fire engines.

These early buyers needed practical, sturdy cars, not gaudy status symbols. Car builders saw the need and rushed to fill it.

Believers in the automobile claimed that it was cheaper to buy and operate than the horse and buggy. According to a 1903 *Scientific American* article, a simple car cost $650 to $1,300 to buy and $25 a month to operate, while a horse and buggy cost up to $1,600 to buy, plus $40 a month for feed, bedding, and medicine. In fact, the automobile was probably no cheaper to buy and run than the horse—but for the same money, it did much more. It went more places in less time, with less trouble. Pioneer car builder Ransom E. Olds summed up the automobile's superiority over the horse. A car, he said, "never kicks or bites, never tires on long runs, and never sweats in hot weather. It does not require care in the stable and only eats while on the road."

Some observers believed the automobile would save America's crowded cities, where—long before the coming of the auto—traffic jams were common. An automobile was half as long as a horse and carriage, they pointed out. It

Ford Model T Delivery Car

Tougher than an army mule and cheaper than a team of horses.

Early Ford advertisements appealed to people looking for an inexpensive, practical car.

could back up more easily and turn in a much narrower circle. Best of all, it did not leave smelly, disease-breeding manure all over the streets. Many city dwellers agreed with the Chicago official who welcomed the automobile with the remark that "ideal health conditions cannot prevail so long as horses are in the city."

By 1907, middle-class people were buying cars, often secondhand. These city and town dwellers were a ripe market for Henry Ford's "universal car." The magazine *Motor Age* reported: "Hundreds of clerks and small businessmen . . . are now to be seen in small cars going to and from their work, instead of being packed in musty streetcars or walking a mile to and from the railroad station."

The automobile made it possible for people to work in the cities without having to live there. City workers who could afford a car could give up their cramped apartments and move to the suburbs. No one could foresee the serious traffic and social problems that this new way of living would cause. The automobile, people thought then, made the American dream—every citizen owning and living on a little piece of American soil—come true.

But the automobile raised new fears and met opposition. It was, then as now, a dangerous machine. On May 30, 1896, Evelyn Thomas of New York City had the dubious honor of becoming America's first auto accident victim, when Henry Wells, driving a Duryea, knocked her off her bicycle. She survived with a broken leg; Wells spent the night in jail.

Before long, newspapers were filled with gruesome stories of automobile accidents. Every day, it seemed, more innocent people were being killed or maimed. Careless drivers hell-bent on speed were attacked in the press and from church pulpits. In 1901, when the speed limit in New York City was eight miles per hour, cars were clocked on Fifth Avenue at speeds of up to twenty-five.

A few cities and towns tried to outlaw automobiles completely, but that approach never worked. By 1906, most states had speed limits of twenty or twenty-five miles per hour on country roads, lower in built-up areas. To make catching speeders easier, cities and states required that cars be registered, with the number displayed on the back of the vehicle—the first license plates. In Chicago, some motorists fought back: To protect their "right" to go as fast as they pleased, they put fake license numbers on their cars.

Licensing of drivers was slower to catch on. Beginning in 1900, Chicago made motorists take a yearly written test. Other cities and states were less strict. In Milwaukee, the only requirement for a license was that the driver be at least eighteen years old and have two arms. In 1907, Massachusetts became the first state to require a road test; for many years after that, most states let drivers get their licenses by mail.

Speed limits and other automobile laws had to be enforced. At first, police

This photo from 1895 shows a traffic policeman on a bicycle catching a "speeding" car on New York City's Fifth Avenue.

were at a disadvantage. An officer on foot or on horseback could not chase a speeder and make him or her pull over. The best the patrolman could do was jot down the license number, look up the owner's name, and track the speeder down later. Under those conditions, it was hard to make a speeding charge stand up in court. The speeder could claim that the officer read the number wrong or that someone else had been driving the car.

So police departments began buying cars of their own, and the chase was on. Another antispeeding device was the speed trap: Concealed in the bushes, officers with stopwatches clocked motorists and popped out to stop those who were going over the limit. To encourage the speeders to stop, police sometimes stretched ropes or cables across the road, or threw logs in the paths of their cars. Motorists resented speed traps; almost every driver had his or her own horror story about being stopped in some little "town that tickets built."

For some Americans—blacksmiths, stable owners, horse breeders—the automobile spelled economic disaster. Those who had foresight (and enough

This early Ford repair shop in New Iberia, Louisiana, was probably a stable before the automobile became commonplace.

money) adapted to changing times. A blacksmith might have fewer horses to shoe, but there were more and more cars for him to repair. Stable owners retired their horses and began garaging, servicing, and renting out cars. Still, some industries were doomed—though the last buggy-whip factory in the nation managed to stay in business until the 1960s.

Sometimes enemies of the automobile took matters into their own hands. In the early 1900s, children in the New York City slums pelted cars with rocks when motorists disrupted their street stickball games. In the country, some citizens declared war on tourists whose cars bothered them and their livestock. The farmers plowed up roads, spread nails or broken glass to flatten tires, and even chased motorists away with shotgun blasts.

But by the time Ford's Model T appeared, farmers, like other Americans, had accepted the automobile. The Master of the New Jersey Grange, a powerful farmers' league, said in 1908: "We farmers are not opposed to the motorcar. . . . It will be an important feature in making farm life more attractive."

The sturdy Model T could go where other cars couldn't, as shown in this 1912 photograph.

More and more farmers bought cars, and by 1910 there were 50,000 on American farms—most of them Model Ts. Ford designed his car to give long service on rough roads. The body rode high off the ground, letting the T cross streams and run on rutted roads that stopped sleek, low-slung cars. Farm families also used the car as a portable power source: They jacked up the rear and ran a leather drive belt from one wheel to whatever machine they wanted to use. Thus, the car churned butter, crushed apples, sawed firewood, and did other chores. When, years later,

the family T finally died, it made a dandy chicken coop.

One farmer wrote: "Before I got my Ford it took me a whole day to get my produce into town. Now I load the rear seat with butter, eggs and vegetables. . . . I can make the trip to town and back by noon, and besides saving half a day's time, I get 20 percent better prices by being to market before the rest."

Besides giving farm families an economic boost, the automobile brought them into closer touch with the world outside. They might not have electricity

Model Ts lined up in front of an early Ford dealership.

or telephones, but once they had a car, country folks were less isolated. They could visit back and forth more easily. If someone fell sick or was injured, the auto was there to rush the patient to a doctor. Going to church was no longer an all-day project. Trips to town were made only when absolutely necessary in the horse-and-wagon days, but they became a weekly routine once the family had a car. Car owners could shop, socialize, and perhaps visit the nickelodeon to take in that other new invention, Mr. Edison's moving pictures.

By 1909, the first full year of Model T production, the United States had 87 million people, 24 million horses and mules, 200,000 automobiles, 233,000 miles of railroad tracks, and just over 2 million miles of roads—most terrible.

Of those 2 million miles of roads, 153,000 were classified as "improved"—graded and spread with gravel. In cities and towns, some major streets were surfaced with brick, cobblestones, or wooden blocks. Elsewhere no roads were paved. In the spring, roads were bottomless pits: Cars bogged down in the thick, soupy, clinging mud. Traffic kicked up choking clouds of dust in dry summer and fall weather, and the rough roads shook cars and the people in them mercilessly. In the winter, ice and snow clogged the roads. Because of poor road quality, it cost 25 cents to move a ton of goods one mile on American roads, compared with 12 cents per mile in Europe.

Car manufacturer Colonel Albert Pope said: "The American who buys an automobile finds himself with this great difficulty: he has nowhere to use it. He must pick and choose between bad roads and worse." Colonel Pope had been agitating for better roads since 1880, long before the coming of the automobile. He was then the nation's largest bicycle manufacturer. Cyclists wanted better roads to go touring on. They joined forces with farmers, who needed better roads to move their products to market. The "good roads" movement made slow progress, even after motorists joined the cause in the early 1900s. Towns, counties, and states began spending more money on roads. Those that could afford it began paving with concrete. But as fast as American roads could be improved, increasing motor traffic tore them up. Therefore, Henry Ford and other successful American manufacturers designed and built rugged cars that could handle roads as they were.

In 1910, fourteen years after his first car ran successfully, auto pioneer Charles Duryea wrote: "The novelty of owning an automobile has largely worn off." Indeed, the automobile had conquered the United States. Cars were everywhere—on city streets and country roads and even out in the wilderness where no roads had yet been built. Most of those Americans who did not yet own cars were just waiting for the price to come within their reach. Thanks to Henry Ford's basic idea—make as many cars as possible and sell them at the lowest price—the price of the Model T dropped steadily, year after year. With every cut in price, more Americans took to the roads, headed for the future.

Within the means of millions

Automobile parking grounds adjacent to factories may be seen today in every American industrial center. They offer a striking proof of the better standard of living that workers in this country enjoy.

Here Ford cars usually outnumber all others. Their low cost and operating economy bring them within the means of millions; and in families where the cost of living is high even in proportion to income, the purchase of a car is possible with little sacrifice through the Ford Weekly Purchase Plan.

FORD MOTOR COMPANY ∴ DETROIT, MICH.

Runabout	. $260	Tudor	. . $580
Touring	. $290	Fordor	. . $660
Coupe	. . $520		

All Prices F. O. B. Detroit

On Open Cars Starter and Demountable Rims $85 Extra. Full-Size Balloon Tires Optional at an Extra Cost of $25.

THE UNIVERSAL CAR

MAKE SAFETY YOUR RESPONSIBILITY

4

FIVE DOLLARS A DAY

The news stunned the United States and the world: Henry Ford would pay his workers $5 for working an eight-hour day. Their pay would more than double: At the time—January 1914—most Ford workers made 26 cents an hour, $2.34 for a nine-hour day. And Ford was one of the better-paying manufacturers in the country.

The move to $5 a day came at a first-of-the year meeting of Henry Ford and his top executives. The company had made a profit of $27 million the year before. Of that profit, $5 million was paid to stockholders as dividends—making Ford, who owned 58 percent of the company's stock, richer than ever.

The men at the meeting knew that 1914 would be an even better year for the company. They expected profits of at least $30 million. Henry Ford believed

By the 1920s, owning a Model T was within the means of millions of American workers, as this ad for the "universal car" shows.

the company should share some of the profits with the men who built the Model T. Standing at a blackboard covered with figures, the story goes, he kept erasing and rewriting the average daily pay for workers: $3, $3.50, $4 . . .

"I dare you to make it $5," growled Ford's business manager, James Couzens. Ford erased once more, chalked in "$5," and that was that—according to Henry Ford's version of the story. After he quarreled with Ford and left the company, Couzens claimed that the $5 day had been *his* idea.

Other manufacturers criticized the $5 day. Ford was spoiling his workers, they said, by paying them more than was good for them. They accused him of trying to steal their best employees. *The Wall Street Journal* called the move "an economic crime"; it was, sniffed *The New York Times*, "foredoomed to failure." Some people complained that women employees were excluded. "We expect the young ladies to get married,"

Workers fit an engine into a Model T chassis in the Ford plant in Highland Park, Michigan.

Ford replied; until they did, he said, they would receive a "proportionate increase." (Two years later, women were fully included in the $5 plan.)

Headlines blazed the story around the world, and people eager to make big pay flocked to Detroit. At 2:00 A.M. on January 6, the day after the announcement, a crowd began gathering outside the Highland Park plant. By the end of the day, 10,000 people were there. A few days later, the crowd numbered 15,000. Newspapers told heartbreaking stories of men who had sold their few belongings to pay for the trip to Detroit. The Ford company was not ready to

deal with this mass of people. Notices went up: There would be no hiring for a month; Detroit residents would get preference for new jobs. But the job seekers kept coming.

Monday, January 12, was bitter cold. Outside the Ford plant, 10,000 people waited, shivering. Ford workers had to push and shove their way into the building. Scuffles broke out, rocks smashed the plant windows, and before anyone realized what was happening, a full-scale riot was on. A handful of policemen struggled to restore order, but they were badly outnumbered. Desperate, they turned fire hoses on the

By 1924, a motorized assembly line was in use at the Highland Park plant.

crowd. In the below-zero weather, the rioters' soaked clothing froze almost instantly. The crowd fled.

If Henry Ford had thought ahead, he might have seen the excitement and possible trouble his $5 a day move would cause. If he had waited to speak out until the company was ready to deal with throngs of people looking for work, the riot could have been prevented. But waiting was not Ford's style. When an idea burst in his head, he usually acted on it right away.

The $5 day, he said at the time, "is neither charity nor wages, but profit sharing and efficiency engineering."

Men would work harder and better, he believed, if they were paid well. Besides, he said, "when you pay men well, you can talk to them." Henry Ford liked to talk with his workers. In the early days of the company, he knew each one by name. He joked with them (exploding cigars were a favorite trick of his), and he got them to do what he wanted not by giving orders but by making suggestions, like "I wonder if we could get this done right away." A willing worker could do well at the Ford plant. Told that the company had no expert on steelmaking, Ford pointed to a man sweeping the floor and replied:

"Make an expert out of Wandersee!" And the floor sweeper became an authority on steelmaking.

But success changes any company. Even in 1906, Henry Ford was too busy and the Ford plant too big for him to know each and every worker. Beginning in 1908, employees wore numbered badges. In 1909, the first full year of Model T production, over 2,000 people were on the Ford payroll. In 1914, the first year of the $5 day, the company had over 14,300 workers.

Not only did Ford have more workers, it had a different kind of worker. In the days before the Model T, crews of ten to twelve workers built Fords and other cars one at a time. Driven by his dream of making and selling cars in huge quantities, Henry Ford worked to change that system. He found that the work went much faster when the workers stayed in one place while cars and parts came to them. And so the moving assembly line came to the automobile industry.

Henry Ford did not "invent" the assembly line, any more than he "invented" the car. Instead, he perfected the system. He divided up the car-making process into hundreds of small steps. Each step was done, over and over, by one worker, who had all the parts and tools he needed within easy reach. Also, the parts were *interchangeable*—a wing nut or a steering wheel or an engine block from one Model T would fit perfectly on any other.

At the beginning of the line, a bare frame began moving forward. As the frame passed each worker, he added something to it. The car grew, piece by piece, as it moved down the line. Some parts of the car, like the engine and transmission, were put together elsewhere in the plant on assembly lines of their own, and brought to the main line.

At the end of the line, the bare frame had become a complete car, ready to have the body dropped on. The Model T at first came in colors: Touring cars were red and roadsters were gray, both with contrasting pinstripes. Later, the cars were painted a handsome dark green. In 1912, Ford announced that from then on customers could have any color they wanted "as long as it is black." The black-only policy, meant to save time and cut costs, continued until the 1920s. Then, to meet competition from General Motors' colorful cars, the T was offered in four colors.

Under the old system of building cars one at a time, Ford found, it took a worker 12½ hours to put together a Ford chassis (the frame, engine, transmission, steering gear, and wheels). In other words, one worker could assemble a chassis in 12½ hours; two workers, in 6¼; 12½ workers, in one hour.

In 1913, an experimental moving assembly line at the Highland Park plant cut the assembly time to just under six hours. By the beginning of 1914, Ford had four assembly lines running, and the time needed to build a car was down to 1 hour and 38 minutes. That year, the factory turned out a record 248,307 Model Ts.

This photo shows wheels being installed on Model T frames at Highland Park.

Before the assembly line, most Ford workers, like their boss, were skilled mechanics—self-taught, perhaps, but skilled and proud of it. But once the assembly line ruled the plant, skill was no longer an advantage. It took almost no training or experience to stand in the same place all day, putting the same nut on the same bolt again and again. By 1914, most of the Ford workers were unskilled men doing monotonous tasks. Critics saw these new-style workers as slaves to the assembly line, stuck in jobs that gave them no pleasure or satisfaction.

Supporters of the system replied that boring work was better than no work at all. At the Ford plant, they added, workers could transfer from department to department until they found jobs they liked.

Their jobs may have been boring, but Ford workers were happy with their pay. Under the $5 a day policy, the turnover rate—the percentage of the work force that left the company and had to be replaced—dropped sharply. The rate for December 1912 was 48 percent; in 1914, it fell to 6.4 percent for the year.

Better pay meant better lives for the

workers. If the head of a family worked for Ford, others in the family did not have to work to add to the family income. Said one man: "My boy don't sell no more papers. My girl don't work in the house of another and see her mother but once in the week no more. Again we are a family." With their fatter pay envelopes, Ford workers could afford to marry, buy their own homes, and feed and dress their children well.

But would they? Many of the Ford workers—in 1914, two-thirds of them—were foreign-born immigrants, mostly from Italy and Eastern Europe. They were unfamiliar with American ways of living. In Detroit and other big cities, they crowded together with others from their home countries and lived in poor, unsanitary housing. That was fine with many employers—the immigrants worked for low wages and seldom made trouble on the job. But Henry Ford wanted his workers to live and think like "good Americans."

Even those born in this country, he saw, needed help and guidance if they were to use their new higher pay to improve their lives. Many of these American-born Ford workers came from farms; many more were poor African Americans who came to Detroit from the South when they learned that Ford hired workers regardless of race. As much as their foreign-born co-workers, these people were not used to life in big industrial cities.

Honestly believing that he knew what was best for his workers, Henry Ford began supervising their private lives. Early in 1914, the Ford Motor Company created a Sociology Department. (Sociology is the study of how groups of people act.) Investigators from the new department visited Ford workers' homes. Their job was to make sure that each worker used his extra income wisely. If the worker did not—if he drank or gambled or sent his children out to work instead of to school; if his home was dirty or his family poorly dressed—he kept his job but lost his share of the company's profits. With help and advice from the Sociology Department, he could mend his ways and get his extra income back. Most workers cooperated, or at least pretended to.

This kind of management, in which an employer tries to influence a worker's life both on and off the job, is called *paternalism*. The system had its good side. Ford offered classes in English to his foreign-born workers and encouraged them to become American citizens. Any Ford employee who wanted to buy a home could get a free appraisal of the property from the company. This saved many from being cheated by real-estate swindlers. Ford opened a mechanics' training school for boys. He set up a savings bank for his workers and later opened stores where they could buy food and clothing at low prices. Ford was one of the first big manufacturing companies to give its workers paid sick leave.

Ford's well-paid workers turned out Model Ts faster and faster. When the $5 day was announced, the company figured the move would cost $10 million in

Henry Ford's friends included some of the nation's most famous people. Shown here, on a camping trip, are inventor Thomas Edison (standing at left, next to Edsel Ford and an unidentified man); nature writer John Burroughs; Henry Ford; and industrialist Harvey Firestone.

additional wages. In fact, the final cost for the first year was under $6 million, because the workers produced more cars each year than the year before. In 1916, there were 32,000 workers, and they produced almost 500,000 Ts.

With the cars rolling out of the Highland Park plant, Henry Ford had little to do. His executives took care of the paperwork and financial details that bored him. His son Edsel, always eager to please "Father," joined the company and, at the end of 1918, became its president (although Henry Ford remained firmly in control). Henry Ford tinkered constantly with the assembly line, always looking for ways to improve the flow of materials to the workers. As for the car itself, that, he felt sure, was pretty much perfect. He did not care to hear suggestions for improving the Model T.

All Ford wanted to do was build and sell more and more cars. He was not interested in money. "I have never known what to do with money after my expenses were paid," he said. "I can't squander it on myself without hurting myself, and nobody wants to do that." Once in the early days of the Model T, Clara Ford found in her husband's pants pocket a check, made out to him, for $75,000. He had forgotten to cash it.

The enormous profits, Henry Ford believed, should be put to work expanding and improving the company. Here he ran up against an obstacle: The other stockholders wanted the profits paid out in dividends, to themselves. The Dodge brothers, for example, invested $10,000 in the Ford Motor Company in 1903. They owned 10 percent of the stock; that entitled them, they said, to 10 percent of the profits. If the company paid out all its 1915 profits to stockholders, the Dodges would get $2.5 million.

These stockholders, in Henry Ford's eyes, were "parasites." None of them was active in running the company. One, a Detroit lawyer, even boasted that he had never ridden in a Model T. They could not outvote Ford, who owned more than half the company's stock, but they could cause him trouble.

In 1916, Ford announced that from then on, dividends would be limited to a paltry $1.2 million a year. All the rest of the profits would be put back into the company. The day after they attended Edsel Ford's wedding, the Dodges sued, charging that Ford was keeping from them the income they deserved. The Dodges were especially angry because they needed the Ford dividends to finance their own automobile company. The lawsuit dragged on until 1919, when a judge ordered Ford to pay a dividend of $19 million to the stockholders.

Fed up, Ford borrowed $75 million from New York and Boston bankers—a group he deeply distrusted—and bought out the other stockholders. He first drove the value of the stock down by announcing that he was leaving Edsel in charge of the company. He would start a new firm, he said, to manufacture a $250 car. The stockholders, frightened that without Henry, the Ford Motor Company was doomed, sold out. Henry Ford, then fifty-seven years old, at last took full control of his company. The Dodge brothers received $12.5 million, not a bad return on their $10,000 investment. Of course, nothing more was heard about the $250 car.

Around the time of the Dodge suit, in 1916, Henry Ford tried his hand at peacemaking. World War I had been raging in Europe since 1914. The war, he said, was started and kept going by "international banking interests" who stood to profit from it. He came to believe that he could help end the fighting. Encouraged by European pacifists, he agreed to finance a "Peace Ship" that would take distinguished representatives from the United States and other neutral countries to Europe for a peace conference.

The United States had kept out of the war, but many Americans, and most

Clara, Henry, and Edsel Ford aboard the "peace ship" Oscar II.

American newspapers, supported Britain and France against Germany. The Ford Peace Ship (actually a chartered Norwegian freighter named *Oscar II*) was a ship of fools, the newspapers said, and Henry Ford was the biggest fool of all. He was mocked and scorned, but Ford stubbornly went ahead. He promised to "get the boys out of the trenches by Christmas." Few leading Americans wanted anything to do with the planned peace conference. The ship set sail with Henry Ford and a group of what the *New York Times* called "crack-brained dreamers" aboard. The delegates fell to squabbling among themselves, and Ford took to his bed with a bad cold.

When the ship reached Norway, just a few days before the Christmas deadline, it was clear that the trip was in vain. The warring nations of Europe were not about to stop fighting and listen to the peace delegates. Henry Ford went home, discouraged, to be greeted by more public mockery. He kept on opposing the war, but when the United States joined the fighting in 1917, he did his duty. The Ford factories made ships, ambulances, trucks, airplane engines, and 2 million steel helmets for U.S. soldiers. At the time, Ford said that he would take no profits from war work, but later—when the company needed cash—he forgot that well-meant promise.

A 1917 tank made by the Ford Motor Company for the U.S. Army.

In 1916, the U.S. Army was sent across the border into Mexico to deal with what Washington called "border bandits." Ford spoke out against that move, as he did against the war in Europe. That brought a blast from the powerful *Chicago Tribune*, which called him an "ignorant idealist," an "anarchist" (a person who wants to overthrow all forms of government), and an "enemy of the nation."

Ford sued for libel. When the case finally came to trial in 1919, the *Tribune*'s lawyers put him on the stand and made a fool of him. He admitted he read very little, and he showed a weak grasp of American history (for example, he gave 1812 as the date of the American Revolution). In the end, Ford won his suit—but the jury awarded him damages of just 6 cents, and he never forgot his humiliation on the witness stand.

As far as book learning goes, Ford was in fact ignorant. "Books muss up my mind," he once said. He was handy with physical things, not with words. He did not think carefully but jumped from idea to idea, always plunging ahead recklessly, ready to try anything to see if it worked. That approach brought him success as a builder of automobiles, but in other fields it led to embarrassing failures. Yet, from the moment of the $5-a-day announcement, Ford was a celebrity. Reporters asked his opinion on everything under the sun. Whether he knew anything about the subject or not, Ford almost always had an opinion, and always gave it.

Smarting from his battle with the *Tribune* and his defeat in a campaign for the U.S. Senate in 1918, Ford decided he needed a newspaper of his own. He took over a dusty country weekly, the

Dearborn Independent, and made it his public platform. Soon the paper was printing 700,000 copies a week. Most went to Ford dealers all over the country, who were ordered to sell the paper to their customers. Each issue included "Mr. Ford's Own Page" (actually written for him by others) where the automaker pushed his pet causes. He opposed smoking, gambling, and drinking, and he urged Americans to return to the old-fashioned virtues he had learned as a boy 50 years before.

Early in his newspaper career, Ford discovered "The International Jew." Like many Americans who grew up in the nineteenth century, Ford had certain firm beliefs, based on ignorance, about the Jewish people. In his mind, they were greedy moneylenders; they dressed and spoke and lived strangely; it was they who killed Jesus Christ. He believed that they controlled the world by controlling its money. Ford came to identify the Jews with the "Wall Street profiteers" and "international banking interests" who he felt were to blame for the World War—and to whom he owed $75 million.

His *Independent* published a forged plan for Jewish rule of the world called *The Protocols of the Learned Elders of Zion*. Articles called for an end to Jewish immigration, and removal of Jews from positions of power in education, business, and politics. The anti-Jewish (anti-Semitic) campaign was based on suspicion and hatred—yet Ford said he had nothing against Jews personally. One of his oldest friends in Detroit was Rabbi Leo Franklin. Each year he gave the

Henry Ford poses in an early Model A for this publicity photo from the late 1920s.

Jewish leader a new Ford. After the anti-Jewish articles began, Rabbi Franklin returned that year's gift. Genuinely surprised, Ford called him up and asked, "What's wrong, Dr. Franklin? Has something come between us?"

After widespread protests, Ford told the editor of his paper early in 1922, "I want you to cut out the Jewish articles." Ford later publicly apologized to the Jewish American community, but the damage had been done. He had smeared innocent people and, again, ended up looking like a fool. But in the early 1920s, that was one of the least of Henry Ford's problems. His "universal car" and his company were in trouble.

AFTERWORD

END OF THE ROAD

By the middle of the 1920s, the automobile had changed the United States forever. The day of the muddy, dusty, bumpy dirt road was ending: The country had 500,000 miles of smooth highways, and more were being built each year. On business and pleasure, people traveled by car and bus. The new highways were dotted with "tourist camps"—ancestors of today's motels—where car-driving vacationers stopped overnight.

The one-room country schoolhouse began giving way to larger schools that served students from a wide area. The children came to school by bus. Their parents drove to work, drove to town to shop, drove the family to church on Sunday.

Around large cities, new suburbs sprang up. People moved to these suburbs and commuted to work by car. On the farm, the gasoline-powered tractor was well on its way to replacing the horse and the mule. Henry Ford was building 100,000 of his Fordson tractors a year. Farmers snapped them up, in spite of the Fordson's bad habit of tipping over backward. The Communist revolutionaries who seized power in Russia eagerly bought 25,000 Fordsons to modernize their country's agriculture.

By 1925, just about any American could own a car. The price of a Model T was below $400. A person who could not afford even that low price could buy a used car for as little as $25. The idea that every American could, and should, be able to jump in a car and drive anywhere—a mile to the movies or 3,000 miles across the continent—became a new part of the American dream.

As more and more workers built more and more cars, and pumped and refined oil to run them, and made roads for them to ride on, the automobile became a key part of the nation's economy.

This Model T rests in a museum display, but a few carefully maintained Ts are still on the road.

The vast interior of the River Rouge plant, shown during construction.

Besides the workers who actually made the cars, many others depended on the auto industry for their living: car salesmen, repairmen, gas-station owners, operators of hotels, restaurants, and roadside attractions. Millions worked in industries that filled the needs of the car builders—iron, steel, glass, tires, upholstery, paint, and many others.

As the industry grew, the number of makers shrank. No longer could a clever mechanic start an automobile company in his garage. With modern methods, it took big money to be successful in the auto business. With his Model T, Henry Ford was the biggest maker and seller of cars in the country in 1920—but he had to share the low-priced car market with others: General Motors' Chevrolet and Buick divisions; Dodge Brothers; Maxwell; Chrysler (newly formed and soon to take over Dodge Brothers); Hudson, and Studebaker.

Ford meant to stay on top. After World War I ended, in 1918, he began building a new, bigger plant on the Rouge River near Detroit. By 1926, the Rouge plant held 80,000 workers. The plant had its own iron and steel mills, so Ford would not have to depend wholly on outside suppliers. Ford-owned ships brought in raw materials—iron ore from Ford mines, timber from Ford sawmills (but no rubber from the vast Ford plantation in Brazil—that was a failure). Ford's railroad, the Detroit, Toledo, & Ironton, nearly bankrupt when Ford took it over, grew rich carrying goods to and from the plant. On the 1,100 acres were ovens that produced fuel for the blast furnaces; a glass plant; even a paper mill to make cardboard for shipping cartons. Besides whole cars, the plant turned out millions of parts that were put together in Ford's thirty-six assembly plants around the country. All those cars flowed out to a nationwide network of 9,800 dealers.

Sadly, the happy time of the $5 day was over. Ford workers were still paid well, but no better than other industrial workers. By 1920, inflation had robbed the Ford employees of their new prosperity. A $5 day's pay then was worth half what it was back in 1914. Ford raised the day's pay to $6, then $7. But as his work force grew, Henry Ford seemed to lose interest in its welfare. The Sociological Department was dropped in 1921. To keep prices low, Ford management tried to squeeze as much work as possible out of the workers on the assembly line. Again and again, the line was speeded up, forcing the workers to work faster.

Workers grumbled, but there was little else they could do. Ford was a nonunion company and Detroit was a nonunion town, so the workers had no organization to fight for their interests. It was not until 1941 that the United Auto Workers Union won the right to represent Ford workers, after a bitter strike.

It was clear, in the mid–1920s, that Ford could keep doing what he had done best since 1909: turn out Model Ts faster than he could sell them. But *could* he keep selling them? The automobile business had changed, and in some important ways, Henry Ford had not kept up with it. Buyers looked for features that Ford did not offer. They wanted cars that started with the push of a button, not by turning a hand crank. They demanded shock absorbers for a smoother ride, and tires they could change wheel and all (on the T, the wheel stayed on the car and the flat tire had to be pried off and replaced—a hard, time-consuming job). Buyers preferred a three-speed sliding gearshift (the "stick shift" of today) to Ford's old-fashioned system of pedals and levers. They wanted little conveniences—speedometers, gas gauges, gas tanks they could fill without lifting up the

The inside of a Ford dealership in the mid-1920s, showing the different Model T types available—including the Model T touring car and truck.

ADVERTISING THE MODEL T

In the T's early years, the Ford Motor Company depended largely on "word-of-mouth" to let people know about the Model T. Ford did run advertisements in news-papers and magazines, but these were usually simple ads stressing how inexpensive and reliable the T was. In the 1920s, however, the T ran into stiff competition from other cars. In order to keep people aware of the Model T, the Ford Motor Company began to run full-color advertisements in popular magazines like the *Saturday Evening Post* and *Good Housekeeping*. In those days, when radio was a novelty and television hadn't yet appeared, magazine ads provided one of the best ways of getting consumers interested in a product. Reproduced on these pages are some of best-known Model T advertisements of the 1920s.

According to this 1925 ad, a Model T is the "key to the wide and healthful out-of-doors."

Many Model T ads described how practical the car was. This ad, however, appeals to people concerned about fashion.

In this ad, a country doctor uses a Model T to visit a remote patient. Doctors were among the first professionals to make use of the Model T.

Dependable as the doctor himself

THE dependability of the Ford car—like that of the family physician who uses it so extensively—has become almost traditional. Instinctively you place a trust in this car rarely, if ever, felt even for a larger, higher-powered automobile. And it is not uncommon to expect from it a far more difficult service.

Such universal faith is the result of Ford reliability proved over a long period of years—years in which quality has grown consistently better, while price has been steadily reduced.

FORD MOTOR COMPANY, DETROIT, MICHIGAN

Ford

THE UNIVERSAL CAR

There are no stay-at-home days now

Before this family owned a Ford car, a rainy day often meant stay at home—even from school. Now, mother's Ford is always available and she prefers to drive it, confident of the reliable performance, ease of parking and control.

Ford economy is a decided advantage: it is not only low in price and running cost but easy to buy. In fact, many women have arranged with Ford dealers to benefit by the Weekly Purchase Plan, making their payments easily out of the household budget.

FORD MOTOR COMPANY, DETROIT, MICH.

Ford

CLOSED CARS

This ad describes Ford's "Weekly Purchase Plan" for prospective buyers. Credit programs like this, plus the car's normal low price, gave millions of people the chance to own a Model T.

Cancel distance & conquer weather

The woman who drives her own Ford Closed Car is completely independent of road and weather conditions in any season.

It enables her to carry on all those activities of the winter months that necessitate travel to and fro—in or out of town. Her time and energy are conserved; her health is protected, no matter how bitterly cold the day, or how wet and slushy it underfoot.

A Ford Sedan is always comfortable—warm and snug in winter, and in summer with ventilator and windows open wide, as cool and airy as an open car.

This seasonal comfort is combined with fine looks and Ford dependability; no wonder there is for this car so wide and ever-growing a demand.

FORD MOTOR COMPANY, DETROIT, MICHIGAN

TUDOR SEDAN, $590   FORDOR SEDAN, $685
COUPE, $525   ALL PRICES F.O.B. DETROIT

CLOSED CARS

The caption to this 1924 ad—"cancel distance & conquer weather"—highlights the Model T's ruggedness.

front seat, windshield wipers, and other features.

Perhaps most important, they wanted speed, comfort, and style. By the standards of 1925, the Model T had none of these. Its top speed was about forty-five miles per hour; other cars whipped along at fifty-five, even sixty. The T—and the people in it—bucked, shook, and rattled. Even with its side curtains down, the car let in dust, rain, and snow. And it looked old-fashioned, with its boxy shape, high wheels, and black-only color scheme.

In its early days, the T was a simple, practical, long-lasting car. Just as the Ford advertisements promised, it "took you there and brought you back." But now, most people wanted more. Other carmakers, especially General Motors's Chevrolet Division, gave them what they wanted—color, comfort, and good looks for not much more money. Perhaps most important, the other companies began bringing out new models every year. That way, the buyer could be sure his or her car was the newest, latest, and best.

Henry Ford could not understand this new attitude. In his mind, the only reason to change his car was to improve it. He made changes when the changes made sense. In 1914, the T got electric headlights and lost its squeeze-bulb horn. In 1917, the muffler was improved to make it less noisy. In 1919, buyers of Fords could have an electric starter as an extra-cost option.

Styling changes came too, though Ford usually fought them. He began making two-door and four-door closed versions of the T, with solid tops and glass side windows. To improve the car's boxy look, fenders were rounded and the radiator was redesigned. Still, the Model T looked a little more clunky and out-of-date every year. To make matters worse, in the 1920s, Ford—then in his sixties—grew more set in his ways. He let his underlings, led by his son Edsel, try minor changes, but he refused to consider any major mechanical improvements. He agreed to advertise his car more aggressively, especially in magazines for women, but he forced his dealers to pick up a big part of advertising costs.

And the competition was catching up. They succeeded by imitating Ford's production methods. Now it began to seem that they would pull ahead of Ford by building up-to-date cars that offered the buyer more. Though Henry Ford tried to ignore them, the numbers were there to see. In 1921, Ford made 56 percent of the cars sold in the United States. In 1925, Ford's share of the market was down to 45 percent and still dropping. In 1922, Ford production went up 27 percent over the year before—but Chevrolet production rose 220 percent. In 1925, for the first time in many years, Ford sales fell from the previous year.

As 1926 began, Ford sales were slow, despite a 1924 price cut that brought the open touring car down to $290. That was a record low price, but it bought a stripped car. Adding an electric starter and removable wheels—standard features on almost all other makes—pushed the price to $380. Ford tried

The Model A of 1928—the car that replaced the Model T.

more price cuts. He lowered the closed Model Ts to $565 and $520, and offered them in colors. For the first time, a price cut did not bring a rise in sales. In June 1926, he tried again. He made the self-starter standard and reduced most models to below $500. Still, sales were slow. Ford's share of U.S. car production plunged to 34 percent.

No one knows exactly when Henry Ford admitted to himself that the Model T was done for. But in May 1927, the Ford Motor Company announced that a new car would replace the T. The next day, the 15-millionth Model T rolled off the assembly line. By the time T production stopped so that Ford plants could get ready to build the new car, 15,458,781 had been built since 1908.

So good was the reputation Henry Ford built with his Model T that before anyone had even seen the new car, the snappy, up-to-date Model A, 400,000 people went to their Ford dealers and made down payments. Some refused to give up on the T. When she heard that no more would be made, a wealthy lady in New Jersey bought seven of them so she would never have to change. For years after the last T was built, Ford made and sold replacement parts. Today, more than eighty years after the T was born, hundreds are still on the road. You can see them, lovingly restored, at antique car shows.

Henry Ford himself summed up the Model T on the day he announced that he would build no more of them: "The Model T was a pioneer," he said. "It had stamina and power. It was the car that ran before there were good roads to run on. It broke down the barriers of distance in rural sections, brought people . . . together, and placed education within the reach of everyone. We are all still proud of the Model T Ford car."

INDEX

Page numbers in *italics* indicate illustrations

SUGGESTED READING

Aird, Hazel B., and Catherine Ruddiman. *Henry Ford: Boy with Ideas*. New York: Macmillan, 1986.

Evans, Arthur N. *The Automobile*. New York: Lerner Publications, 1985.

Harris, Jacqueline L. *Henry Ford*. New York: Franklin Watts, 1984.

Hokanson, Drake. *The Lincoln Highway: Main Street Across America*. Iowa City: University of Iowa Press, 1988.

Lacey, Robert. *Ford: The Man and the Machine*. Boston: Little, Brown, 1986.

Lewis, David. *The Public Image of Henry Ford: An American Folk Hero and His Company*. Detroit: Wayne State University Press, 1976.

Miller, Ray , and Bruce McCalley. *From Here to Obscurity: The Illustrated History of the Model T Ford*. New York: Evergreen Press, 1971.

Purdy, Ken W. *Motorcars of the Golden Past*. New York: Galahad Books, 1966.

Picture Credits

About the Author

Christopher Simonds grew up in Minnesota. He worked for several newspapers and magazines, taught middle school English for twelve years, and now lives in upstate New York with his wife and two teenaged daughters. He is managing editor of the *Columbia County Independent* and is also the author of *Samuel Slater's Mill* in the *Turning Points in American History* series.